FRANCESCA CAVALLO

FASTEST WOMAN ON EARTH

THE STORY OF TATYANA MCFADDEN

Illustrated by *Luis San Vicente*

undercats

EDITORIAL DIRECTOR: Francesca Cavallo
STORY: Francesca Cavallo
ILLUSTRATIONS: Luis San Vicente
GRAPHIC DESIGN: Francesca Pignataro

Fastest Woman on Earth: The Story of Tatyana McFadden is published by Undercats, Inc. a small independent publisher with a big mission: radically increase diversity in children's media and inspire families to take action for equality.

To see more of our books and download bonus materials and free stories, come visit us at www.undercats.com.

Printed in Canada

At Undercats, we do our best every day to minimize our carbon footprint. We printed this book using FSC® certified materials only, and we always make sure to print at plants that are close to our distribution centers to reduce carbon emissions due to transportation.

Dear Reader,

Tatyana McFadden's story of hope and possibility, perseverance and courage, drive and dedication should inspire all of us. Raised in an orphanage, adopted by a loving American family, and given the freedom to pursue her dreams without limitation, Tatyana is a gift to the world: an educated and accomplished athlete who just happens to be in a wheelchair.

I am writing this introduction from a personal perspective... I am her Mother. I first met this child on a business trip to Russia while serving as the Commissioner for Disabilities during the administration of President George Bush. I was immediately taken by the twinkle in her eye and her "I can do it myself" attitude. That first meeting changed my life as much as Tatyana's.

Born with a disability myself — and a lifelong advocate for people with disabilities — I had never experienced the challenges that parents face as they view the world through the eyes of their son or daughter who has a disability. Tatyana gave me that gift. I hope in reading this book that you, too, will embrace people with disabilities with a heightened awareness of the challenges they face each and every day.

Thank you, Undercats for sharing the story of Tatyana McFadden, my wonderful daughter!

Deborah L. McFadden
Former Commissioner of Disabilities
President and Founder of Competitive Edge
Tatyana's Mom

To the kids and grown-ups
who do things their own way.

ONCE UPON A TIME,

a very poor woman left a baby on the doorstep of a big grey building in Russia.

At House 13, there were many children,
but no moms or dads.

House 13, in fact, was a house where kids
who did not have parents went to live together.

Every morning, the women working at House 13
washed the kids with a hose
and then fed them a cabbage and potato soup.

Day after day, soup after soup,
the kids grew up.

When the other babies in House 13 started to walk,
Tatyana realized that she could not walk like them.
While her friends walked on their feet,

Tatyana had to walk on her **HANDS.**

Tatyana had a condition called *spina bifida*.
Her legs did not support her.
While her friends climbed trees using their arms
and their legs, Tatyana only used her arms.

Over time, she became incredibly

STRONG!

Often, visitors came to House 13.

Sometimes, when those visitors left,
one of the children would leave with them.

That meant the child had been adopted.

From that moment on, the child would have parents,
and the visitors would have a daughter or a son.

Tatyana would get sad when her friends left.

She didn't know if she would ever see them again.

She didn't even know where they
were going to live—she had never been
outside of House 13.

One day, House 13 got a very special visitor named Deborah.

Deborah came from a far-away place called America, and her visit got everyone excited.

House 13 became sparkling clean,
and all the children wore their best clothes.

TATYANA MCFADDEN

Tatyana McFadden has 17 Paralympic medals, seven of them gold; and 24 World Major Marathon wins. At the Paralympic Games in Rio in 2016, she was named the Best Female Athlete by the United States Olympic/Paralympic Committee and was honored as the top female athlete in the world for her outstanding performance, overcoming adversity, and exemplifying sportsmanship.

In 2020, she worked as a producer and star of *Rising Phoenix*, the documentary film that tells the story of the Paralympic Movement through the lives of nine Paralympic athletes.

Tatyana is actively involved in advancing the rights of people with disabilities. She played a key role in passing the Maryland Fitness and Athletics Equity for Students with Disabilities Act, thanks to which students with disabilities now have equal access to compete in interscholastic athletics throughout the United States.

Tatyana received her master's degree in Education from the University of Illinois, as well as an undergraduate degree in Human Development and Family Studies. She lives and trains in Florida. She has a dog named Bentley!

Learn more at
tatyanamcfadden.com.

FRANCESCA CAVALLO is an award-winning, New York Times best-selling author, entrepreneur and activist. She co-created the *Good Night Stories for Rebel Girls* book series and podcast and was the recipient of the Publisher's Weekly StarWatch Award in 2018. In 2019, she parted ways with Rebel Girls, which she had co-founded, to start Undercats, Inc. Francesca's work has been translated into more than 50 languages, and her books have sold more than 5 million copies worldwide.

Instagram: @francescatherebel

LUIS SAN VINCENTE has illustrated more than 40 books. His work has been recognized by various illustration contests around the world. Luis lives and works in Mexico City.

Instagram: @luis_sanvicente_ilustrador

Undercats is a small, independent publisher with a big mission:
radically increase diversity in children's media and inspire families around the world
to take action for equality. We are a female led, LGBTQ+ owned company
with a very diverse team spread across two continents.

For us, books are opportunities to create human connections. We'd love to connect with you,
which is why we created our newsletter "Goodnight Tonight."
Sign up if you want to receive free, monthly bedtime stories celebrating some
of the most beautiful things happening in the world right now.

www.undercats.com/goodnight

Let us know what you think about this book!

Instagram: @undercatsmedia Twitter: @undercatsmedia